Scorpions

by Steven Otfinoski

mc

Marshall Cavendish
Benchmark
New York

animalsanimals

Special thanks to Donald E. Moore III, associate director of animal care at the Smithsonian Institution's National Zoo, for his expert reading of this manuscript

Published by Marshall Cavendish Benchmark
An imprint of Marshall Cavendish Corporation

Other Marshall Cavendish Offices:
Marshall Cavendish International (Asia) Private Limited, 1 New Industrial Road, Singapore 536196 ● Marshall Cavendish International (Thailand) Co Ltd. 253 Asoke, 12th Flr, Sukhumvit 21 Road, Klongtoey Nua, Wattana, Bangkok 10110, Thailand ● Marshall Cavendish (Malaysia) Sdn Bhd, Times Subang, Lot 46, Subang Hi-Tech Industrial Park, Batu Tiga, 40000 Shah Alam, Selangor Darul Ehsan, Malaysia

Marshall Cavendish is a trademark of Times Publishing Limited

All websites were available and accurate when this book was sent to press.

Library of Congress Cataloging-in-Publication Data
Otfinoski, Steven.
Scorpions / by Steven Otfinoski.
p.cm.—(Animals animals)
Includes index.
Summary: "Provides comprehensive information on the anatomy, special skills, habitats, and diet of scorpions"—Provided by publisher.
ISBN 978-0-7614-4878-5 (print)
ISBN 978-1-60870-620-4 (ebook)
1. Scorpions—Juvenile literature. I. Title.
QL458.7.O84 2012
595.46—dc22
2010016035

Cover photo: Thomas Marent/Minden Pictures

The photographs in this book are used by permission and through the courtesy of:
Alamy: iconsight, 7; Peter Arnold, Inc., 10; Photoshot Holdings Ltd., 15; Charles Melton, 24; L. Kennedy, 26; Keith Dannemiller, 30; Robert Clay, 32; Animals Animals - Earth Scenes: Paul & Joyce Berquist, 9; Roger De La Harpe, 16; Corbis: alt-6/plainpicture, 36-37; Getty Images: National Geographic, 1; Paulo De Oliveira, 35; Minden Pictures: Michael & Patricia Fogden, 12; Mark Moffett, 20; Piotr Naskrecki, 21, 23; Photo Researchers Inc.: Babak Tafreshi, 4; Francesco Tomasinelli, 8; Sinclair Stammers, 18, 28; SuperStock: age fotostock, 11.

Editor: Joy Bean
Publisher: Michelle Bisson
Art Director: Anahid Hamparian
Series Designer: Adam Mietlowski
Photo research by Joan Meisel

Printed in Malaysia (T)
1 3 5 6 4 2

Contents

1
Killer with a Sting

In Greek mythology, Orion was the greatest of hunters. He hunted down and killed every creature on the earth. But the creature that finally ended Orion's life was not a ferocious bear or lion. It was a tiny animal with a deadly stinger—a scorpion. It stung Orion on the heel of his foot, killing him. To honor the great hunter, the Greek gods placed Orion in the heavens as a *constellation*, a group of stars. They also honored the scorpion that killed him by making it a constellation, too. But the gods placed the two constellations apart, so they would never fight each other again.

People are as fearful of and fascinated by scorpions today as they were in ancient times. Their fears are mostly groundless. Of the more than 1,300 *species* of scorpions, only about twenty-five have a sting that could kill a human.

The scorpion resembles a crab with a long body, four pairs of legs, and pincers, but it is neither a *crustacean* nor a insect. It is a member of the animal class called *arachnid*, which also includes spiders, mites, and ticks.

The first scorpions appeared on earth more than 450 million years ago, long before the dinosaurs. They lived in the sea and grew to a length of 6.5 feet (2 meters). These sea scorpions were among the first animals to crawl out of the sea and onto dry land. They *evolved* into the first land scorpions, which were much smaller and closely resemble scorpions today.

There are two parts to a scorpion's body. The first part, the *cephalothorax*, is composed of the head and chest, or *thorax*. It has a pair of claws, or *pincers*, it uses to catch *prey* and as many as seven pairs of eyes. The second part, the *abdomen*, is composed of the main part of the body and a tail. The scorpion's long body contains the lungs,

Did You Know . . .
Scorpio—the scorpion—is one of the twelve signs of the *zodiac*, another creation of the ancient Greeks. People born between October 23 and November 21 are under the sign of Scorpio.

The two parts of a scorpion can be seen clearly: the head and chest, and the abdomen and tail.

digestive system, and sex organs. Like the cephalo-thorax, the abdomen is protected by a hard, bony outer layer called a *carapace*. The abdomen has four pairs of legs that the scorpion walks on. The long, segmented tail ends in a stinger, which it uses to inject *venom* into prey or an enemy to paralyze it.

Species Chart

An African scorpion.

◆ The African scorpion, also known as the imperial or emperor scorpion, is the largest of all scorpions. It grows to more than 8 inches (20 centimeters) in length and can weigh almost 2 ounces (56.7 grams). It lives in the forests of West Africa and eats insects and small animals such as mice.

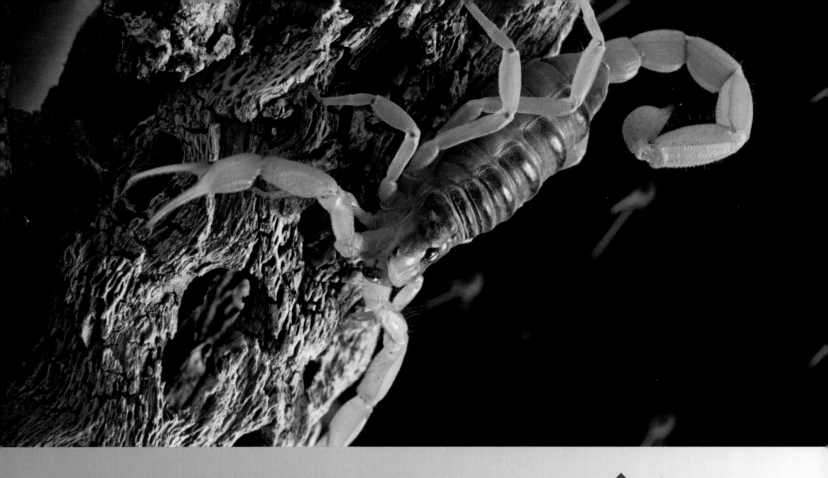

An Arizona hairy scorpion.

◆ The Arizona hairy scorpion, also known as the giant scorpion, is one of the largest found in North America. It grows to a length of 5 to 6 inches (12.7 to 15.2 cm) and lives in the desert regions of Mexico, western Arizona, Southern California, and parts of Nevada and Utah. It gets its name from the thick, brown hairs that cover its body. It eats lizards, snakes, and even other scorpions.

A striped scorpion.

◆ The striped scorpion (also called the striped bark scorpion) is the most common scorpion in the United States. It is one of the smaller scorpions and adults are typically between 1 and 2.5 inches (2.5 to 6 cm) long. It is found in a number of states, including Texas, Oklahoma, Kansas, and New Mexico.

Scorpions are yellow or black in color and range from under 1 inch (2.5 cm) to 8 inches (20 cm) in length. Females and males look very much alike, although the females are a little fatter.

Scorpions live all over the world except on the *continent* of Antarctica, the Arctic region, and the island nation of New Zealand. There are about ninety species of scorpions found in North America, with some living as far north as southern Canada. No scorpions are found east of the Mississippi River. Scorpions prefer living in warm climates, although some have adapted to chillier surroundings. Deserts are their favorite habitat, but they also thrive in grasslands and tropical rain forests.

A scorpion's stinger has venom, which it can inject into enemies and prey.

2 A Powerful Predator

Scorpions eat all kinds of insects and spiders. Larger species will consume animals such as mice, lizards, and snakes. Just as Orion hunted for his food, so does the scorpion. Most scorpions are *nocturnal predators*. They do this because the deserts in which many of them live are very hot during the day, a time when it is too hot for any activity. Despite all their eyes, scorpions do not see well, especially in the dark. They rely on the sensitive *bristles* on their feet and underneath their abdomen to tell them when prey is near. The bristles feel the vibrations an insect or small animal makes as it moves along the ground. As the vibrations grow stronger, meaning the insect or animal is getting closer, the scorpion remains completely still. When the

A dune scorpion eats a dune cricket.

prey is very close, the scorpion strikes. It grabs the prey with its fore pincers and holds it tightly. If the prey is a small insect, the scorpion will kill it with its pincers, but if it is a bigger insect, such as a cricket or an animal such as a mouse or lizard, it uses its stinger to subdue the creature. The scorpion's venom is stored in a *sac* underneath the stinger. The scorpion sticks the sharp end of its stinger, called a *telson*, into the prey's skin. Muscles pump the venom from the scorpion's sac through the stinger into the open wound. In a matter of seconds, the victim is paralyzed and cannot move.

Now the scorpion has a problem. Its mouth is not built for chewing food, so it must find another way to eat its prey. It spits strong digestive juices from its mouth onto its prey. The juices act like acid, melting the prey into a sticky liquid that the scorpion then can drink with its mouth.

This process of reducing its prey to liquid can take hours, but the effort is worth it. One good meal can satisfy the scorpion for several months. It does not need to drink water often since it gets moisture from the

Did You Know . . . .
All adult scorpions have a substance on their bodies that makes them glow a greenish yellow under ultraviolet light. Scientists looking for scorpions at night will often shine an ultraviolet lamp on the ground to find them.

14

A scorpion can kill its prey with its sharp pincers.

In order to eat its food, a scorpion will spit digestive juices from its mouth onto its prey:

prey's body. This is an important survival tool since there is very little water in the desert. The scorpion will drink water occasionally when it can find it, such as when there is morning dew on plants.

Scorpions usually live alone. When they meet up with another scorpion, they are more likely to fight than befriend one another. These fights can often be to the death. Sometimes the victor, if it has not eaten in a while, will devour the other scorpion.

3

A Dangerous Courtship

Few animals have as complicated—or dangerous—a courtship ritual as scorpions. The male and female find each other, usually at night, by releasing chemical signals called *pheromones*. Once they locate each other, they approach one another over open ground. They appear to be more rivals than animals looking for a mate. Their mating dance closely resembles a wrestling match and may last from minutes to days, depending on the species. In some species, the male scorpion may rub the female with his tail and even sting her! In other species, the male will seize the female's claws in his own. Sometimes he will entwine his tail with hers. The male does this for a good

A male whip scorpion holds on to a female whip scorpion during a courting ritual.

19

reason—survival. The female, once they mate, may decide to sting the male to death and eat him to provide nourishment for the babies growing inside her!

When the moment is right for mating, the male will scrape a hollow area in the ground with his feet and deposit his *sperm* in a packet called a *spermatophore*. He then guides the female over the hollow area so she can take the packet into her body. Once she has done so, the male usually makes a fast retreat. His job is done, but he still fears the female may try to eat him.

A female wind scorpion eats the head of her suitor.

The female raises her young entirely on her own. The young are born any time from several months up to a year and a half after the female becomes pregnant, depending on the species of scorpion. The babies are born inside the mother—inside a tough skin covering that she breaks open using her stinger. She delivers them standing erect on two pairs of hind legs. As they emerge from her body, she catches the young in two pairs of front legs that she holds together. Her *brood* may number from twenty-four to one hundred. The newborns are colorless, but otherwise look like miniature adults. They immediately climb onto her back and cling to her with their tiny pincers. They will remain there for about two weeks as they

This scorpion mother carries her young on her back, where they are protected by her stinger.

grow bigger and gain strength. They are also protected on her back from predators that would devour them if they were on their own.

At the end of the two weeks, the young begin to *molt*, or shed their skin for a larger body. Each time they molt, their body increases in size by 20 to 40 percent. Now they are ready to climb off their mother's back and live on their own. In about seven months, some of the young are ready to mate and start their own families.

In the wild, scorpions live between two and six years. Some may live up to ten years or even longer.

Did You Know . . .
Young scorpions molt up to seven times before reaching their full size as adults.

22

This whip scorpion, which has just molted, will be vulnerable for a few hours until its outside hardens.

The Hunter Hunted

Scorpions are fearless predators, but they are also prey for a number of other animals. Frogs, salamanders, lizards, snakes, bats, some mice, owls, insects, such as the praying mantis, and black widow spiders all prey on scorpions.

If attacked, some species of scorpion make clicking or buzzing noises to warn the predator they have a stinger and will use it. However, some of these creatures are willing to risk being stung by the scorpion's stinger to get a chance to eat its tasty body. Others, such as the South American camel spider, will first try to bite off the scorpion's tail, which contains its stinger, making the scorpion all but defenseless.

An owl holds on to a scorpion it has caught as a meal.

A meerkat eats a scorpion.

26

Two predators—a certain kind of frog and a mammal called the meerkat—are *immune* to the venom of some scorpions. Scorpions are a regular part of the meerkat's diet. In desert areas where most meerkats live, the animal digs in the sand looking for scorpions. When a meerkat finds one, it does not know if its venom can hurt it. So the meerkat hits the scorpion over the head with a paw to stun it. If the meerkat moves fast enough, the scorpion does not have time to sting it. The meerkat then grabs the scorpion by its tail and eats it or feeds it to its young. Adult meerkats teach their young how to hunt and kill scorpions. Scorpions are also prey for other scorpions that are larger than themselves.

To avoid being attacked, the scorpion will hide during the day underground in a burrow it digs and sometimes lives in. It may also hide under a rock or in the cracks of dry desert earth.

Scorpions have adapted to different environments just as they have adapted to avoiding predators. While most species live in hot or warm areas, some have adapted to living in forests and woodlands.

27

Did You Know . . .
There is an old legend that says if a scorpion is cornered by a predator, it will sting itself to death rather than be killed by the predator. Today we know this legend has no basis in fact.

A scorpion hides under a rock to keep out of the strong rays from the sun.

28

They make their homes under pieces of tree bark and rocks or in logs or leaf litter. Some even manage to survive in cold, mountainous regions in South America and Asia. They do so by *hibernating* during the coldest months of the year. They settle down under rocks or in burrows in the ground. Their body processes slow down, and they require little or no food to stay alive. As soon as the weather grows warmer, the scorpions become active again and go out to hunt for prey. One scientist froze scorpions in his laboratory and then thawed them out in the sun. They came back to life and walked away. In a similar way, scorpions can become inactive during the hottest months of the year in deserts, a process known as an *estivation*, which is an inactive state and a survival technique similar to hibernation in the wintertime. During the hottest hours of the day, scorpions will rest where it is cool, such as under rocks or in burrows.

29

Scorpions and People

Most scorpions have little to fear from people, but many people are very afraid of scorpions. This fear, especially in North America, is largely groundless. Scorpions may look as if their sting would pack a big punch, but the vast majority of scorpion stings are no more harmful to humans than the sting of a bee or wasp. The pain and swelling from the scorpion sting can be treated with an ice cube or a cold compress and painkillers. The pain normally disappears within twenty-four hours. However, people can be allergic to a scorpion sting, just as they can be to a bee sting. If the allergy is severe, the person stung can become seriously ill or, in rare cases, even die.

Dr. Luis Possani is working on developing a serum to fight the poisons in a scorpion's sting.

Scorpion stings do happen in the United States, but they are rarely fatal.

32

The only truly deadly scorpion in the United States is the tiny bark scorpion that lives in the Arizona desert. Like most scorpions, it shies away from humans, so people are seldom stung by it. The last person to die from a sting of a bark scorpion in the United States occurred in 1964. However, since then, several other people have died from the stings of other scorpions, some that were mistakenly brought into the United States from other countries in cargo and luggage.

Only about thirty to forty of the two thousand species of scorpions worldwide are dangerous to humans. But they account for about five thousand *fatalities* each year, and that's about ten times the number of deaths from poisonous snake bites. In Mexico alone, a thousand to two thousand people die of scorpion stings annually. Many of the sting victims are children and elderly people whose bodies are less resistant to the venom. Many of these deaths occur in poor countries or remote areas where people do not have ready access to *antivenin*, an antidote that can counteract the venom if administrated soon after the stinging takes place.

Among the most venomous of scorpions are the yellow scorpion of Brazil and several varieties of fat-tailed scorpions found in the Middle East and Africa. One kind of fat-tailed scorpion can spray its venom in the air up to a distance of 2 feet (61 cm). If the venom gets into a person's eyes, it can cause temporary blindness. If not washed out quickly, the venom can cause permanent damage to the eyes.

One way to tell if a scorpion is particularly poisonous is to look at the size of its pincers. The bigger the pincers, the less the power of the scorpion's venom. Scorpions with big pincers can easily grab and kill their prey and do not need to sting it. Many of them also live in deep underground burrows where they can safely avoid predators. Scientists believe that over time these scorpions will lose their venom and the ability to produce it. They may even evolve to the point where they will have no stinger or tail.

Believe it or not, some people keep scorpions as pets! The most popular pet species is the emperor, or imperial, scorpion. It is quiet, clean and easy to care for. It is also

Did You Know . . . .
The deadliest of all scorpions is the Sahara scorpion, also known as the death stalker. It is found in North Africa and the Middle East, and its venom can kill a human within a few hours.

Some people keep scorpions as pets, and this emperor scorpion is the most popular kind of scorpion to keep as a pet.

The imperial scorpion is considered endangered. There are fewer imperial scorpions around because they are losing their habitat due to so many trees being cut down where scorpions live.

less aggressive than other species of scorpions. Other scorpions that make good pets include African burrowing scorpions, fat rock scorpions, gold scorpions, and Asian forest scorpions.

If you are thinking about buying a scorpion for a pet, first make sure that it is legal in your state. You will want to keep your scorpion in a *terrarium* with a secure lid, as you would with a snake or other reptile. Like pet snakes, scorpions require artificial light and artificial heat. Put 3 to 6 inches (7.6 to 15 cm) of soil or peat at the bottom of the terrarium for burrowing. Scorpions also like a rock or piece of bark to hide under and require water in a shallow dish and live, well-fed insects, such as crickets or mealworms, to eat. You can have more than one scorpion as pets, but be sure you provide enough food so they don't fight or eat each other. You can handle your scorpion once in a while, but be careful! It may sting you.

Most species of scorpions are not *endangered.* Scorpions reproduce quickly and have large populations. Some people see them as pests, but if left alone, they actually do good by eating harmful insects. But a few species are threatened with extinction. The imperial scorpion is endangered because so many members of this species have been captured for the pet trade. Other scorpion species threatened by over collecting for the pet trade are the flat rock scorpion, the burrowing scorpion, and the creeping scorpion, all found in South Africa. Other factors endanger these species as well. The imperial scorpion is also endangered due to an increasing loss of its habitat— the rain forest, which is being cut down for farming and building. The burrowing scorpion will only make its burrows in certain kinds of soils. Human development has removed some of these soils and narrowed the scorpion's range. Unlike many species of scorpions, the flat rock scorpion has a low reproductive rate and a long birthing period. At least three other scorpion species have been listed by the Convention on International Trade in Endangered Species of Wild Fauna and Flora (CITES). Laws were passed in 1995 making the trade of these scorpion species illegal.

Most of us will never see a scorpion outside of a zoo, and maybe that is a good thing. Yet these legendary animals have captured our imagination for thousands of years and continue to fascinate us today.

Glossary

abdomen—The rear part of a scorpion's and many insects' bodies.

antivenin—Medicine given to a person stung by a scorpion to stop the venom from working in the body.

arachnid—An animal class whose members have eight legs, including spiders, scorpions, and ticks.

bristles—Sensitive hairs on an animal's body.

brood—A group of offspring produced at one time.

carapace—Hard, protective exoskeleton layer of a scorpion's body.

cephalothorax—One of the two body segments of the scorpion, containing the head and chest.

constellation—A group of related stars that appear to form the shape of a person, animal, or thing from Greek mythology.

continent—One of the world's seven large landmasses.

crustacean—A class of animals having a hard outer shell, including lobsters and crabs.

endangered—Facing possible extinction.

estivation—An inactive state some animals enter to survive during hot summers.

evolved—Adapted; changed over time.

fatalities—Deaths resulting from a disaster.

hibernating—Going into a deep sleep for the winter, something certain animals do to survive the cold and scarcity of food.

immune—Protected from a disease.

molt—To shed old skin to make way for growth and new skin on an animal's body.

nocturnal predator—An animal that is active at night and preys on, or kills and eats, other animals to survive.

pheromones—Chemicals released by scorpions and other animals to help identify one another or to communicate in other ways with creatures of the same species.

pincers—Claws on scorpions, crabs, and other animals.

prey—An animal that is hunted and eaten by other animals.

sac—A baglike structure inside an animal's body.

species—A group of animals that share the same characteristics and mate only with their own kind.

sperm—A male reproductive cell.

spermatophore—A capsule surrounding a mass of sperm produced by a male scorpion.

telson—The stinger at the end of a scorpion's tail.

terrarium—A glass tank for keeping certain pet animals such as scorpions, reptiles, and amphibians.

thorax—The chest part of a scorpion's or insect's body located between the head and the abdomen.

venom—A poisonous fluid that scorpions and some snakes inject into their prey to paralyze and kill it or to defend themselves.

zodiac—An imaginary belt in the heavens that includes twelve constellations, or signs.

Find Out More

Books

Lunis, Natalie. *Stinging Scorpions* (No Backbone! the World of Invertebrates). New York: Bearport Publishing, 2009.

Mcfee, Shane. *Scorpions* (Poison!) New York: PowerKids Press, 2007.

Pringle, Laurence. *Scorpion Man: Exploring the World of Scorpions.* New York: Aladdin, 2008.

Rubio, Manny. *Scorpions* (A Complete Pet Owner's Manual). Hauppauge, NY: Barron's Educational Series, 2008.

Thomas, Isabel. *Scorpion vs. Tarantula* (Animals Head to Head). Chicago: Heinemann-Raintree, 2007.

Websites

A-Z Animals
http://a-z-animals.com/animals/scorpion/

Animal Planet
http://animaldiscovery.com/invertebrates/scorpion/

Desert USA
www.desertusa.com/oct96/du_scorpions.html.

Enchanted Learning
www.enchantedlearning.com/paint/subjects/arachnids/scorpion/Scorpionprintout.shtml

Index

Page numbers for illustrations are in **boldface**.

About the Author

Steven Otfinoski is the author of more than a dozen books in the Animals Animals series, including *Koalas, Hummingbirds, Dogs, Horses, Skunks, Jaguars,* and *Raccoons.* Otfinoski lives in Connecticut with his wife, a high school teacher and editor.